Say it in
Greek 2

The Phrase Book

A simple way for English-speaking children
to learn how to speak Greek

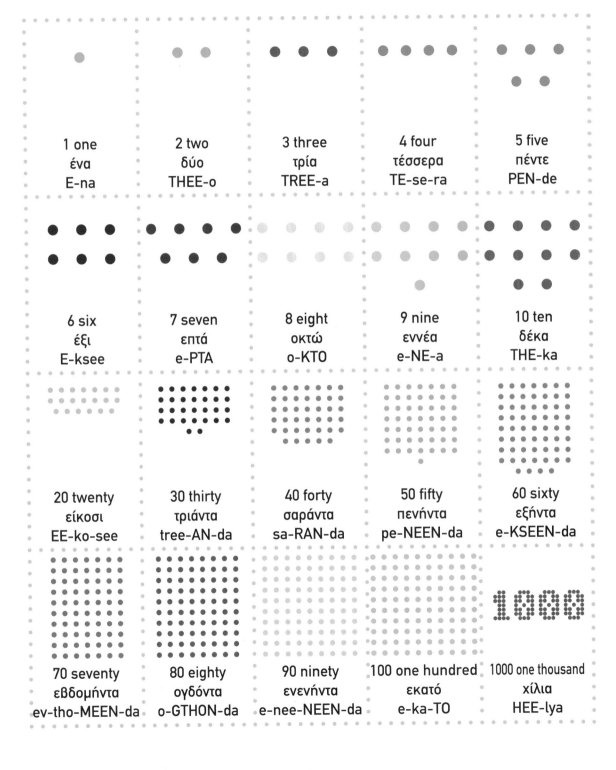

1 one ένα E-na	2 two δύο THEE-o	3 three τρία TREE-a	4 four τέσσερα TE-se-ra	5 five πέντε PEN-de
6 six έξι E-ksee	7 seven επτά e-PTA	8 eight οκτώ o-KTO	9 nine εννέα e-NE-a	10 ten δέκα THE-ka
20 twenty είκοσι EE-ko-see	30 thirty τριάντα tree-AN-da	40 forty σαράντα sa-RAN-da	50 fifty πενήντα pe-NEEN-da	60 sixty εξήντα e-KSEEN-da
70 seventy εβδομήντα ev-tho-MEEN-da	80 eighty ογδόντα o-GTHON-da	90 ninety ενενήντα e-nee-NEEN-da	100 one hundred εκατό e-ka-TO	1000 one thousand χίλια HEE-lya

PRONUNCIATION GUIDE

Each dictionary entry includes a guide with English letters to show how Greek words are pronounced. Greek words have accents, to reflect. That capital letters are used in the accented syllable. Some Greek sounds can not be replicated exactly in English. Please refer to the guide below to help you pronounce the words correctly.

• When you see an "α" in this guide, it is pronounced in Greek as "ah" or "aa", as in the word "father".
• The letter, "β", is pronounced like the English letter, "v", as in the word "vote."
• The Greek "γ" has a soft "g" sound. It does not sound like the "g" in the word "gate," for example. It's a soft, gutteral "g" from the back of the throat, that almost sounds like a "y", in the word "yes." For simplicity, we use the letter "g" in the guide in most cases, except when it sounds like an English "y". In those cases, we use the letter "y".
• The Greek "δ" has a soft sound, closer to the "th" in the English word "the" or "then." We also use the letter "d" to reflect the sound made whenever you see the following two letters: "ντ."
• An "ε" in this guide is pronounced in Greek like the "e" in the word "elephant."
• When an "ee" is used in the guide, it is pronounced in Greek like the "e"-sound in the words "read" or "weed."
• the Greek, "θ", is pronounced like the English "th" as in the word "think."
• the Greek "μπ" is pronounced like an English "b."
• the Greek "x" is pronounced like an English "h."
• the Greek "σx" combines an "s" and a hard "h" in English, but it is not the "shhh" sound that we get in English. Both letters are pronounced so we use "s(ho)" to indicate that you need to pronounce both the "s" and the "h" separately.

GREETINGS

Καλημέρα.
Ka-lee-ME-ra.
Good morning.

Καλησπέρα.
Ka-lee-SPE-ra.
Good evening.

Καληνύχτα.
Ka-lee-NEE-hta.
Good night.

Τι κάνετε;
Tee KA-ne-te?
How are you?

Καλά ευχαριστώ. Εσύ;
Ka-LA ef-har-ee-STO. e-SEE ?
Fine, thanks. You?

Είμαι πολύ καλά!
EE-me po-LEE ka-LA!
I am very well!

Τι κάνεις;
Tee KA-nees?
How are you?

Τι κάνετε;
Tee KA-ne-te?
How are you?

Είμαι καλά.
EE-me ka-LA.
I am fine.

Είμαστε καλά.
EE-ma-ste ka-LA.
We are fine.

5

Γεια σου!
YA-soo!
Hello!

Πώς τα περνάς;
POS ta per-NAS?
Are you having a good time?

Περνάω υπέροχα.
Per-NAO ee-PE-ro-ha.
I'm having a great time.

Εντάξει. Αντίο.
en-DA-ksee. a-DEE-o.
Ok. Good-bye.

Πρέπει να φύγω τώρα.
PRE-pee na FEE-go TO-ra.
I have to go now.

QUESTIONS

Πώς σε λένε;
POS se LE-ne?
What's your name?

Πόσο χρονών είσαι;
PO-so hro-NON EE-se?
How old are you?

Που μένεις;
poo ME-nees?
Where do you live?

Σε ποια τάξη πηγαίνεις ;
se pya TA-ksee pee-YE-nees?
What grade are you in ?

Με λένε Μαρία.
me LE-ne Ma-REE-A.
My name is Maria.

Είμαι έξι χρονών.
EE-me E-ksee hro-NON.
I am six years old.

Μένω στην Αστόρια.
ME-no steen
a-STO-ree-a.
I live in Astoria.

Πηγαίνω στην τρίτη τάξη.
pee-YE-noo steen TREE-tee TA-ksee.
I am in third grade.

EXPRESSIONS

11

FEELINGS

Σε αγαπώ πολύ.
se a-ga-PO po-LEE.
I love you very much.

Είμαι στεναχωρημένη.
EE-me ste-na-ho-ree-ME-nee.
I am sad.

Είμαι στεναχωρημένος.
EE-me ste-na ho-ree-ME-nos.
I am sad.

Είμαι χαρούμενος.
EE-me ha-ROO-me-nos.
I am happy.

Είμαι χαρούμενη.
EE-me ha-ROO-me-nee.
I am happy.

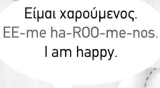

Είμαι θυμωμένος.
EE-me thee-mo-ME-nos.
I am angry.

Φοβάμαι.
fo-VA-me.
I am scared.

Είμαι θυμωμένη.
EE-me thee-mo-ME-nee.
I am angry.

Περαστικά.
pe-ra-stee-KA.
Get well.

Είμαι άρρωστος.
EE-me A-ro-stos.
I am sick.

Είμαι άρρωστη.
EE-me A-ro-stee.
I am sick.

13

15

MY FAMILY

Αυτή είναι η οικογένειά μου.
af-TEE EE-ne ee ee-ko-YE-nee-A moo.
This is my family.

Αυτός είναι ο μπαμπάς μου.
af-TOS EE-ne o ba-BAS moo.
This is my father.

Αυτός είναι ο αδελφός μου.
af-tos EE-ne o a-thel-FOS moo
This is my brother.

Αυτή είναι η μαμά μου.
af-TEE EE-ne ee ma-MA moo.
This is my mother.

Αυτή είναι η αδελφή μου.
af-tee EE-ne ee a-thel-FEE moo
This is my sister.

Έχω δυο ξαδέλφια.
e-HO THEE-o ksa-THEL-fya.
I have two cousins.

Έχω μια θεία και έναν θείο.
e-HO MEE-a THEE-a ke e-NAN THEE-o.
I have one aunt and one uncle.

ACTIVITIES

Πλένω το πρόσωπό μου.
PLE-no to PRO -so-PO moo.
I am washing my face.

Τι κάνεις τώρα;
tee KA-nees TO-ra ?
What are you doing now?

Βουρτσίζω τα δόντια μου.
voor-TSEE-zo   ta THON-dya moo.
I am brushing my teeth.

Πίνω το γάλα μου.
PEE-no to GA-la moo.
I am drinking my milk.

21

Είναι εφτά το πρωΐ.
Είναι ώρα να σηκωθείς .
EE-ne e-FTA to pro-EE.
EE-ne O-ra na see-ko-THEES.
It is seven in the morning.
It is time for you to get up.

Πρέπει να πας σχολείο.
PRE-pee na pas s(h)o-LEE-o.
You have to go to school.

Είναι εννέα και μισή το βράδυ.
Είναι ώρα να κοιμηθείς.
EE-ne e-NE-a ke mee-SEE to VRA-thee.
EE-ne O-ra na kee-mee-THEES.
It is 9:30 at night.
It is time for you to go to bed.

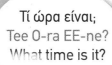

Τί ώρα είναι;
Tee O-ra EE-ne?
What time is it?

Είναι οχτώ
EE-ne o-KTO.
It is eight o'clock.

Είναι μία και τέταρτο
EE-ne MEE-a ke TE-tar-to
It is one fifteen.

Είναι έξι και μισή.
EE-ne E-ksee ke mee-SEE.
It is six thirty.

Είναι δώδεκα παρά τέταρτο.
EE-ne THO-the-ka pa-RA TE-tar-to.
It is a quarter to twelve.

DAYS OF THE WEEK

Σήμερα είναι Σάββατο.
SEE-me-ra EE-ne SA-va-to.
Today is Saturday.

Αύριο είναι Κυριακή.
AV-ree-o EE-ne kee-ree-ya-KEE.
Tomorrow is Sunday.

Χθες ήταν Παρασκευή.
(h)THES EE-tan pa-ra-ske-VEE.
Yesterday was Friday.

Δευτέρα
the-FTE-ra
Monday

Τρίτη
TREE-tee
Tuesday

Τετάρτη
te-TAR-tee
Wednesday

Πέμπτη
PEMP-tee
Thursday

Παρασκευή
pa-ra-ske-VEE
Friday

Σάββατο
SA-va-to
Saturday

Κυριακή
kee-ree-ya-KEE
Sunday

Καλή αρχή.
ka-LEE ar-HEE
Happy start.

Το σχολείο αρχίζει
τον Σεμπτέμβριο.
To s(h)o-LEE-o ar-HEE-zee
ton sep-TEM-vree-o.
School starts
in September.

Καλά Χριστούγεννα.
ka-LA hree-STOO-ye-na.
Merry Christmas.

Καλή χρονιά.
Ka-LEE hro-NYA.
Happy New Year.

Τα Χριστούγεννα
είναι τον Δεκέμβριο.
Ta hree-STOO-ye-na EE-ne
ton the-KEM-vree-o.
Christmas is in December.

Χριστός Ανέστη.
hree-STOS a-NE-stee.
Christ has risen.

Καλό Πάσχα.
ka-LO PA-s(h)a.
Happy Easter.

Χρόνια Πολλά.
HRO-nya po-LA.
Happy Nameday
(literally "many years").

Χαρούμενα γεννέθλια.
Να τα εκατοστήσεις.
ha-ROO-me-na ye-NE-thlee-a.
na ta e-ka-to-STEE-sees.
Happy Birthday.
May you live to be 100!

* The months
of the year often
are shortened
in conversation.
MAR-tee-os, for
example, becomes
simply MAR-tees
or MAR-tee.

Ιανουάριος
ee-A-noo-A-ree-os
January

Φεβρουάριος
fev-roo-A-ree-os
February

Μάρτιος
MAR-tee-os
March

Απρίλιος
a-PREE-lee-os
April

Μάϊος
MA-ee-os
May

Ιούνιος
ee-OO-nee-os
June

Ιούλιος
ee-OO-lee-os
July

Αύγουστος
AV-goo-stos
August

Σεπτέμβριος
sep-TEM-vree-os
September

Οκτώβριος
o-KTO-vree-os
October

Νοέμβριος
no-EM-vree-os
November

Δεκέμβριος
the-KEM-vree-os
December

SEASONS

O χειμώνας
O hee-MO-nas
Winter

Δεν μου αρέσει πολύ ο χειμώνας.
den mou a-RE-see po-LEE o hee-MO-nas
I don't like the winter very much.

Η Άνοιξη
ee A-nee-ksee
Spring

Λατρεύω την άνοιξη.
la-TRE-vo teen A-nee-ksee.
I adore spring.

Το καλοκαίρι
To ka-lo-KE-ree
Summer

Μου αρέσει πολύ το καλοκαίρι.
moo a-RE-see po-LEE to ka-lo-KE-ree.
I like the summer very much.

Το φθινόπωρο
To fthee-NO-po-ro
Autumn

Αγαπώ το Φθινόπωρο.
a-ga-PO to fthee-NO-po-ro.
I love the fall.

29

WEATHER

31

Πού είναι η βιβλιοθήκη;
POO EE-ne ee vee-vlee-o-THEE-kee?
Where is the library?

Στρίψε αριστερά.
STREE-pse a-ree-ste-RA.
Turn left.

Στρίψε δεξιά.
STREE-pse the-ksee-A.
Turn right.

Προχώρα ευθεία.
Pro-HO-ra ef-THEE-a.
Go straight ahead.

Μπορώ να έχω
το μολύβι σου παρακαλώ;
bo-RO na E-ho to mo-LEE-vee
sou pa-ra-ka-LO?
Can I use your pencil please?

...το βιβλίο σου;
to vee-VLEE-o soo?
your book?

...τη γόμα σου;
tee GO-ma soo?
your eraser?

...το ψαλίδι σου;
to psa-LEE-dee soo?
your scissors?

...την κόλλα σου;
teen KO-la soo ?
your glue?

33

AT CHURCH

Κάθε Κυριακή πάμε στην εκκλησία.
KA-the kee-ree-ya-KEE PA-me steen
e-klee-SEE-a.
Every Sunday we go to church.

Στην εκκλησία ανάβουμε κερί.
Steen e-klee-SEE-a   a-NA-voo-me ke-REE.
At church we light a candle.

Προσκυνούμε τις εικόνες
και κάνουμε τον σταυρό μας.
Pro-skee-NOO-me tees ee-KO-nes
ke KA-noo-me ton sta-VRO mas.
We kiss the icons and we make
the sign of the cross.

35

WITH FRIENDS

Τι γίνεται;
Tee YEE-ne-te?
What's up?

Όλα καλά.
O-la ka-LA.
All good.

Τί είναι αυτά;
Tee EE-ne af-TA?
What is that?

Είναι τα παιχνίδια μου.
EE-ne ta peh-NEE-thya moo.
These are my toys.

Είναι πολύ ωραία.
EE-ne po-LEE o-RAY-a.
They are very nice.